FAST
FINGER
FOOD

Your Promise of Success

KÖNEMANN

Food to go

These recipes are designed with speed and convenience in mind. They're home-cooked fast food, which can be eaten without formality by people in a hurry. Perfect for substantial family snacks, many recipes can double as party food, and they are especially suitable for young people with hearty appetites.

Tangy Tomato Dip with Pita Crisps

Preparation time:
  15 minutes
Total cooking time:
  10 minutes
Makes 2 cups

2 tablespoons oil
1 onion, chopped
2 cloves garlic, crushed
2 small red chili
  peppers, chopped
1 16-ounce can whole
  tomatoes, crushed
2 tablespoons chopped
  pimiento
2 tablespoons lemon
  juice
⅓ cup chopped parsley
3 pita bread pockets
¼ cup sour cream

1. Preheat oven to moderate 350°F. Heat oil over medium heat in a medium saucepan. Add onion, garlic and chili peppers to pan. Cook and stir for 2 minutes or until the onion is tender.
2. Add tomatoes, pimientos and lemon juice. Bring to a boil; reduce heat. Simmer, uncovered, for 5 minutes or until reduced and thickened. Stir in parsley.
3. Split pita pockets in half horizontally. Cut each round into eight triangles. Place in single layer on a baking sheet. Bake 10 minutes or till golden brown and crisp.
4. Spoon dip into bowl; top with sour cream. Serve warm or cold, as a dip for pita crisps.

Note: Pimientos are roasted red bell peppers, bought in jars.

Tangy Tomato Dip with Pita Crisps.

Deviled Chicken Wings

Preparation time:
 5 minutes
Total cooking time:
 45 minutes
Serves 4

½ *cup tomato sauce*
¼ *cup Dijon mustard*
2 *tablespoons*
 Worcestershire sauce
2 *teaspoons dried*
 oregano, crushed
1 *onion, finely*
 chopped
2 *cloves garlic*
 crushed
12 *chicken wings*

1. Preheat oven to moderately hot 425°F. Combine tomato sauce, mustard, Worcestershire sauce, oregano, onion and garlic in a large baking dish. Add chicken wings; stir until chicken is well coated.
2. Bake for 45 minutes or until chicken is golden brown. Turn chicken occasionally and brush with mixture during cooking.

Variation: Use chicken drumsticks if more convenient, but allow extra cooking time.

Crispy Samosas

Preparation time:
 20 minutes
Total cooking time:
 4 minutes each batch
Makes 16

2 *sheets frozen puff*
 pastry, thawed.
oil for deep-frying

Filling
8 *ounces ground pork*
 or veal
1 *medium carrot, finely*
 grated
½ *cup frozen tiny peas,*
 thawed
2 *cloves garlic, crushed*
2 *teaspoons curry*
 powder
2 *tablespoons tamarind*
 sauce (see Hint)

1. Roll each pastry sheet into an 11 x 11-inch square. Cut each sheet into four squares. Cut each square into two triangles.
2. *To make Filling:* In a medium saucepan cook ground meat until brown; drain off fat. Stir in remaining ingredients.
3. Divide filling evenly between pastry triangles. Brush edges of pastry with a little water. Fold pastry over to enclose filling and form small triangles. Press edges together to seal.
4. Heat oil to 375°F in a deep heavy-based pan. Gently lower small batches of samosas into hot oil. Cook for 4 minutes or until golden and crisp, turning occasionally. Carefully remove from oil with tongs or slotted spoon. Drain on paper towels; keep warm. Repeat with remaining samosas. Serve with a bowl of chutney.

Note: Have the oil deep enough to allow the samosas to float.

HINT
Tamarind sauce is an acidic Asian sauce that can be found in Asian food shops, supermarkets or specialty food stores. Cakes of tamarind pulp are also available. Dissolve the pulp in hot water and strain. Lemon juice is a good substitute.

Deviled Chicken Wings (top) and Crispy Samosas.

Sesame Shrimp with Tangy Mint Chutney

Preparation time:
 20 minutes
Total cooking time:
 2 minutes per batch
Serves 4

24 large or jumbo
 uncooked shrimp
1/3 cup all-purpose flour
1 egg, lightly beaten
3/4 cup fine dry bread
 crumbs
1/2 cup sesame seeds
oil for deep-frying

Tangy Mint Chutney
1 cup fresh mint leaves,
 firmly packed
2/3 cup fruit chutney
3 tablespoons lemon
 juice

1. Peel shrimp, leaving
tails intact. Cut shrimp
down the back and
devein. Flatten shrimp
slightly.
2. Toss shrimp in flour;
shake off excess. Dip
shrimp in beaten egg
and coat with combined
bread crumbs and
sesame seeds.
3. Heat oil to 375°F in
a deep, heavy-based
pan. Gently lower
shrimp into hot oil.
Cook for 2 minutes or
until golden brown,
turning occasionally.
Carefully remove from
oil with tongs or a
slotted spoon. Drain on
paper towels.
4. *To make Tangy
Mint Chutney:*
Combine mint, chutney
and lemon juice in a
blender or food
processor bowl. Process
for 15 seconds or until
smooth. Serve as a dip
for shrimp.

Sesame Shrimp with Tangy Mint Chutney.

Peel and devein shrimp, leaving the tails intact. Flatten slightly.

Dip shrimp into beaten egg and coat with combined bread crumbs and seeds.

Cook shrimp in hot oil for 2 minutes or until golden brown, turning occasionally.

For *chutney*, process mint, chutney and lemon juice until smooth.

Beef Satay Skewers with Quick Peanut Sauce

Preparation time:
  15 minutes
Total cooking time:
  12 minutes
Serves 4

1 pound boneless beef
  round steak
1 tablespoon oil
1 tablespoon honey
1 tablespoon soy sauce

Quick Peanut Sauce
⅔ cup peanut butter
2 tablespoons soy sauce
½ cup water
1 tablespoon sweet chili
  sauce

1. Trim meat of excess fat; cut into thin strips. Thread meat onto eight short bamboo skewers. Combine oil, honey and soy sauce in small bowl.
2. Place meat on lightly oiled broiler pan; brush with oil mixture. Broil 4 inches from the heat for 12 minutes or until desired doneness; brush with oil mixture occasionally and turn once. Serve warm with peanut sauce.

3. *To make Quick Peanut Sauce:* Place peanut butter, soy sauce, water and chili sauce in a small saucepan. Stir over medium heat until smooth.

Feta Triangles

Preparation time:
  20 minutes
Total cooking time:
  15 minutes
Makes 8

2 teaspoons oil
1 small onion, finely
  chopped
10 ounces fresh spinach
1 cup shredded
  mozzarella cheese
4 ounces feta cheese,
  crumbled
1 egg, lightly beaten
2 sheets frozen puff
  pastry, thawed

1. Preheat oven to 425°F. Heat oil in large heavy-based saucepan over medium heat. Add onion and cook for 3 minutes or until soft. Transfer to large mixing bowl. Remove stems from spinach; wash thoroughly. Place damp spinach leaves in pan. Cover and cook over medium heat for 1–2 minutes or until just wilted. Do this in two batches, shaking pan often and lifting leaves with tongs to evenly wilt spinach. Set aside to cool.
2. Take handfuls of wilted leaves and squeeze out as much moisture as possible. Chop and add to bowl. Add mozzarella and feta cheese; mix well. Add egg and stir until well combined.
3. Roll each sheet of pastry into an 11 x 11-inch square. Cut each pastry sheet into four squares. Divide mixture between squares; fold over to form triangles. Place on baking sheets. Bake 15 minutes or until golden. Serve warm or cool.

Beef Satay Skewers with Quick Peanut Sauce (top) and Feta Triangles.

> HINT
> When cooking meat on bamboo skewers, soak the skewers in water for 30 minutes before using. This will prevent them from burning.

Spring Rolls

Preparation time:
 25 minutes
Total cooking time:
 10 minutes
Makes 8

8 ounces ground pork
2 small carrots,
 coarsely shredded
2 green onions, finely
 chopped
2 ounces Chinese
 cabbage, finely
 shredded
2 ounces bean sprouts,
 coarsely chopped
1 small red bell pepper,
 cut into short thin strips
2 cloves garlic, crushed
1 teaspoon grated fresh
 gingerroot
8 large spring roll
 wrappers
oil for deep-frying
soy sauce, to serve

1. Cook pork in a heavy-based skillet over medium heat for 5 minutes or until brown. Remove meat with a slotted spoon and set aside to cool slightly.

2. Place vegetables, garlic and gingerroot in a large mixing bowl; use hands to combine thoroughly. Transfer to skillet and stir-fry for 2 minutes until soft. Combine vegetables and meat in a large bowl; mix well.

3. Working one at a time, place spring roll wrapper diagonally on work surface. Place about ½ cup of mixture across front half of wrapper. Fold the corner closest to you back over filling. Tuck in sides and roll up. Moisten corner with water to secure. Repeat with remaining filling and wrappers.

4. Heat oil to 375°F in a medium heavy-based saucepan. Gently lower spring rolls into hot oil. Cook over medium-high heat for 1–2 minutes or until crisp and golden. Cook only one or two at a time. Carefully remove with tongs or slotted spoon. Drain on paper towels. Serve warm with soy sauce.

> HINT
> You can buy spring roll wrappers in Asian or large supermarkets. If you don't use the whole package, the rest can be frozen. Once defrosted, they should be kept in the refrigerator.

Spring Rolls.

When pork is browned, remove from pan with a slotted spoon.

Use your hands to combine thoroughly the vegetables, garlic and gingerroot.

Tuck in end and sides of spring roll
wrapper and roll up.

Gently lower spring rolls into hot oil, one
or two at a time.

Cheesy Corn Muffins

Preparation time:
  10 minutes
Total cooking time:
  20 minutes
Makes 12

1 cup all-purpose flour
¾ cup cornmeal
1 tablespoon sugar
2 teaspoons baking
  powder
¼ teaspoon baking soda
⅛ teaspoon salt
1 cup shredded cheddar
  cheese
1 7-ounce can corn,
  well drained
2 eggs, lightly beaten
⅔ cup milk
2 tablespoons oil

1. Preheat oven to moderate 350°F. Brush muffin cups with melted butter or oil.
2. Stir together flour, cornmeal, sugar, baking powder, baking soda and salt in large bowl. Add cheese and corn. Make a well in the center. Pour combined eggs, milk and oil into well.
3. Using a wooden spoon, stir until ingredients are just combined. Do not overbeat. Spoon mixture into prepared muffin cups. Bake for 20 minutes, until puffed and golden. Remove from pan immediately and serve warm.

Mini Corn Dogs

Preparation time:
  10 minutes
Total cooking time:
  1 minute per batch
Makes 16

8 frankfurters
8 wooden skewers
cornstarch for dusting
oil for deep-frying
catsup for dipping

Batter
1 cup all-purpose flour
¾ cup cornmeal
1½ teaspoons baking
  powder
¼ teaspoon salt
1 egg, lightly beaten
¾ cup water
2 tablespoons oil

1. Cut frankfurters crosswise in half. Cut skewers in half. Insert a skewer into each frankfurter. Dust lightly with cornstarch.
2. **To make Batter:** Sift flour, baking powder and salt into a medium mixing bowl; make a well in the center. Add combined egg, water and oil gradually. Stir until smooth (batter will be thick).
3. Heat oil to 375°F in a deep heavy-based pan. Holding the skewers, dip frankfurters into batter a few at a time; allow excess batter to drip off. Using tongs or a slotted spoon, gently lower frankfurter dogs into oil. Cook for 3 minutes or until golden and crisp and heated through, turning occasionally with tongs. Carefully remove from oil. Drain on paper towels; keep warm. Repeat with remaining frankfurters. Serve with catsup as a dip.

Note: The skewers are left in the frankfurters during cooking.

HINT
For extra flavor, add 1 teaspoon of chopped fresh chili pepper or a pinch of chili powder to the corn dog batter.

Cheesy Corn Muffins (top) and Mini Corn Dogs.

Vegetable Fritters

Preparation time:
  30 minutes
Total cooking time:
  3 minutes each batch
Serves 4–6

1 egg
1 cup water
1 cup all-purpose flour
4 ounces broccoli
1 small onion
1 small carrot
1 small red bell
  pepper
oil for deep-frying

1. In a large mixing bowl stir together egg and water. Add flour and beat with a whisk until smooth. Cover bowl with plastic wrap and refrigerate for 10 minutes.
2. Cut broccoli into small flowerets. Finely slice onion, and cut bell pepper and carrot into thin strips. Add vegetables to batter; stir to combine.
3. Heat oil to 375°F in a medium heavy-based pan. Using tongs, pick up two or three pieces of batter-coated vegetables at a time and lower into oil. Hold vegetables in oil a few seconds until batter begins to set and vegetables hold together. Release from tongs and cook until crisp and golden, 2 to 3 minutes. Drain on paper towels and serve with sweet chili or soy sauce.

Salmon Patties

Preparation time:
  20 minutes
Total cooking time:
  6 minutes
Serves 4

2 6¾-ounce cans
  boneless, skinless
  salmon
1 medium potato
1 green onion, finely
  chopped
1 tablespoon fine dry
  bread crumbs
1 egg, lightly beaten
2 tablespoons oil

Quick Tomato Salsa
1 medium tomato,
  finely chopped
1 green onion, finely
  chopped
1 clove garlic, crushed
1 tablespoon finely
  chopped parsley
2 teaspoons red wine
  vinegar

1. Drain salmon thoroughly and place in a large mixing bowl. Flake with a fork. Grate potato, squeeze out excess liquid; add to salmon. Add green onion, bread crumbs and egg to bowl; mix well.
2. Divide mixture into eight portions and shape into patties about 2¾ inches in diameter. Heat oil in a skillet and cook patties over medium heat for 3 minutes on each side or until golden. Serve with tomato salsa.
3. *To make Quick Tomato Salsa:* Place tomato, green onion, garlic, parsley and wine vinegar in a medium mixing bowl and combine thoroughly.

HINT
To save time, use purchased bottled salsa instead of making it yourself. Salsa can be found in the Mexican section of supermarkets, in mild, medium and hot varieties.

Vegetable Fritters (top) and Salmon Patties.

Corn and Potato Cakes

Preparation time:
  15 minutes
Total cooking time:
  4 minutes per batch
Makes about 20

2 large potatoes,
  peeled, grated
1 8-ounce can corn
  kernels, drained
4 eggs, lightly beaten
²/₃ cup fine dry bread
  crumbs
6 green onions, chopped
¼ teaspoon each salt,
  pepper, ground cumin,
  ground coriander,
  ground cinnamon
¼ cup oil

Dipping Sauce
1 8-ounce container
  plain yogurt
3 tablespoons chopped
  fresh mint
2 teaspoons sweet chili
  sauce

1. Drain grated potato on paper towel, squeeze out excess moisture.
2. Combine potato in a medium bowl with corn, eggs, bread crumbs, green onions and spices. Mix well.
3. Heat two tablespoons of the oil in a heavy-based skillet over medium-high heat. Drop heaping tablespoons of mixture into skillet. Cook for 2 minutes on each side or until golden brown. Drain on paper towels; keep warm. Repeat with remaining mixture. Add extra oil to pan if necessary.
4. *To make Dipping Sauce:* Combine all ingredients. Mix well. Serve with cakes.

Crispy Cheese and Lentil Balls

Preparation time:
  15 minutes
Total cooking time:
  1 minute per batch
Makes about 30

1 cup red lentils
4 green onions, chopped
2 cloves garlic, crushed
1 teaspoon ground
  cumin
1 cup fresh bread crumbs
1 cup shredded cheddar
  cheese
1 large zucchini, finely
  shredded
1 cup cornmeal
oil for deep-frying

1. Place lentils in a medium saucepan; cover with water. Bring to a boil; reduce heat. Cover and simmer for 10 minutes or until lentils are tender. Drain; rinse under cold water.
2. Combine half the lentils in a food processor bowl or blender with green onions and garlic. Using the pulse action, press button for five seconds or until mixture is pulpy. Transfer to a large bowl; add remaining lentils, cumin, bread crumbs, cheese and zucchini, stir until combined.
3. Using hands, roll level tablespoons of mixture into balls, toss lightly in cornmeal.
4. Heat oil to 375°F in a heavy-based saucepan. Gently lower small batches of mixture into hot oil. Cook for 1 minute or until golden brown, crisp and heated through, turning occasionally. Carefully remove from oil with tongs or a slotted spoon; drain on paper towels. Repeat with remaining mixture. Serve hot.

Note: These are delicious served with chutney or yogurt as a dip.

*Corn and Potato Cakes (top)
and Crispy Cheese and Lentil Balls.*

Fried Calamari with Tartar Sauce

Preparation time:
 20 minutes
Total cooking time:
 1 minute per batch
Serves 4

1 pound calamari
 (squid), cleaned
¼ cup cornstarch
2 eggs, lightly beaten
2 cloves garlic, crushed
2 teaspoons grated
 lemon peel
1 cup fine dry bread
 crumbs
oil for deep-frying

Tartar Sauce
1 cup mayonnaise
2 tablespoons chopped
 chives
2 tablespoons chopped
 dill pickle
1 tablespoon seeded
 mustard

1. Slice calamari thinly. Toss calamari in cornstarch; shake off excess. Dip into combined egg, garlic and lemon peel. Coat with bread crumbs; shake off excess.
2. Heat oil to 375°F in a deep heavy-based saucepan. Gently lower small batches of calamari into hot oil. Cook for 1 minute or until just heated through and lightly browned. Carefully remove from oil with a slotted spoon. Drain on paper towels; keep warm. Repeat with remaining calamari.
3. **To make Tartar Sauce:** Combine mayonnaise, chives, pickles and mustard. Mix well. Serve as a dip.

Vegetable Pastry Shells with Creamy Pesto

Preparation time:
 15 minutes
Total cooking time:
 8 minutes
Serves 4

Creamy Pesto
⅔ cup firmly packed
 fresh basil leaves
¼ cup heavy cream
¼ cup grated Parmesan
 cheese
1–2 tablespoons oil
1 clove garlic, crushed

Vegetable Filling
2 tablespoons oil
1 small onion, cut in
 wedges
4 ounces cherry
 tomatoes, halved
4 ounces button
 mushrooms, sliced
½ avocado, peeled and
 chopped
1 tablespoon balsamic
 vinegar

4 frozen puff pastry
 shells

1. Preheat oven to moderate 350°F.
To make Creamy Pesto: Combine basil, cream, cheese, oil and garlic in a food processor or blender. Process for 20 seconds or until mixture is smooth and creamy. Transfer to small bowl; cover with plastic wrap.
2. **To make Vegetable Filling:** Heat oil in a medium saucepan over medium heat. Add onion and cook for 1 minute or until soft. Add cherry tomatoes and mushrooms; cook for 1 minute or until just tender. Add chopped avocado and vinegar; remove pan from heat.
3. Place frozen pastry shells on a baking sheet and bake according to package directions. Spoon some warm vegetable filling into each shell and top with a little pesto. Serve immediately.

Fried Calamari with Tartar Sauce (top) and Vegetable Pastry Shells with Creamy Pesto.

Lamb Kebabs with Mango Relish

Preparation time:
  15 minutes
Total cooking time:
  10–15 minutes
Serves 4

1 *pound boneless lamb*
4 *green onions*
1/3 *cup hoisin sauce*

Mango Relish
1 *tablespoon oil*
1 *onion, chopped*
2 *small red chili*
  peppers, chopped
1 *large mango, peeled,*
  chopped
2 *tablespoons white*
  wine vinegar
2 *tablespoons sugar*

1. Trim lamb of excess fat. Cut lamb into 1-inch cubes. Cut onions into 1-inch pieces. Thread lamb and onions alternately onto bamboo skewers. (Soak skewers for 30 minutes before using.)

2. Place kebabs onto a cold, lightly oiled broiler pan. Brush with hoisin sauce. Broil 4 inches from the heat for 4 minutes on each side or until cooked as desired, brushing occasionally with hoisin sauce.

3. *To make Mango Relish:* Heat oil over medium heat in a medium saucepan. Add onion and chili peppers; cook and stir for 2 minutes or until onion is tender. Add mango, vinegar and sugar. Bring to a boil; reduce heat. Simmer, uncovered, for 5 minutes or until mixture has a pulpy consistency. Serve with lamb kebabs.

Note: Use a bottled chutney or relish as a shortcut.

HINT
For this recipe, you could use lamb rib chops or another lean cut of lamb. Another option is to ask your butcher to bone a leg of lamb for you, and to cut it into 1-inch cubes.

Do not overcook the lamb. Although traditionally served well done, it is becoming most acceptable to serve lamb slightly pink and the result is a moister and more tender meat.

Lamb Kebabs with Mango Relish.

Chili Burgers

Preparation time:
15 minutes
Total cooking time:
10 minutes
Makes 4

½ cup canned red
   kidney beans
8 ounces ground pork
   sausage
2 tablespoons tomato
   paste
1 onion, finely chopped
1½ teaspoons chili
   sauce
1 teaspoon ground
   cumin
4 round bread rolls

Topping
1 avocado, chopped
1 small green bell
   pepper, chopped
1 medium ripe tomato,
   chopped
½ cup shredded
   cheddar cheese
⅓ cup sour cream

1. Place beans in a
medium bowl; mash
slightly with a fork.
Add sausage, tomato
paste, onion, chili sauce
and cumin; stir until
combined. Divide
mixture into four; press
into flat patties.
2. Place patties on a
cold, lightly oiled broiler
pan. Broil 4 inches
from the heat for 3
minutes on each side or

until golden brown and
cooked through.
3. **To make Topping:**
In a small bowl,
combine avocado, bell
pepper, tomato, cheese
and sour cream.
4. Split rolls in half; toast
lightly under broiler.
Place patties on bottom
half of rolls and spoon
topping over patties. Top
with remaining rolls.

Burgers with the Works

Preparation time:
   20 minutes
Total cooking time:
   16 minutes
Serves 4

1¼ pounds ground beef
1 medium onion, finely
   chopped
1 tablespoon
   Worcestershire sauce
2 tablespoons tomato
   sauce
½ cup fine dry bread
   crumbs
1 egg, lightly beaten
2 teaspoons oil
4 slices cheddar cheese
4 sesame seed
   hamburger buns
4 lettuce leaves
1 medium tomato, sliced
4 slices canned beets
tomato or barbecue
   sauce

1. Place beef, onion,
sauces, bread crumbs
and egg in a large
mixing bowl. Using
hands, combine mixture
thoroughly. Divide into
four equal portions and
shape into patties about
½ inch thick.
2. Heat skillet and brush
lightly with oil. Cook
burgers over medium-
high heat for 8 minutes
each side, turning once.
Place a slice of cheese
on top of each burger
for the last 4 minutes
of cooking.
3. While burgers are
cooking, cut buns in
half horizontally and
toast lightly under the
broiler. Place lettuce,
tomato and beets on
each bun; top with
burger. Add tomato or
barbecue sauce, place
top half of bun on top.
Serve immediately.

Note: Try sliced
pineapple, grilled
bacon or fried egg on
burgers.

HINT
Make up a double
quantity of burger
mixture and freeze
one batch for future
use. Form into
patties; separate with
plastic wrap and
place in a plastic bag.

Chili Burgers (top) and Burgers with the Works.

Lamb Burgers with Cheese and Bacon

Preparation time:
15 minutes
Total cooking time:
6 minutes
Makes 4

1 *pound ground lamb*
1 *onion, finely chopped*
2 *teaspoons fresh chopped rosemary*
¼ *cup tomato paste*
4 *slices bacon*
4 *slices cheese*
4 *sesame seed hamburger buns*
2 *tablespoons Dijon mustard*
1 *medium carrot, finely shredded*
1 *cup finely shredded lettuce*

1. Combine lamb, onion, rosemary and tomato paste in a medium bowl. Divide mixture into four; shape into flat burgers.
2. Wrap a bacon slice around each burger; secure with a toothpick.
3. Place on a cold, lightly oiled broiler pan. Broil 4 inches from the heat for 3 minutes on each side or until cooked through. Place a slice of cheese on each burger;

remove from heat. Remove toothpick.
4. Split hamburger buns in half; grill on each side until lightly toasted. Spread base of buns with mustard; top with burgers, carrot and lettuce. Place top of bun on top. Serve.

Chick Pea and Ricotta Burgers

Preparation time:
15 minutes
Total cooking time:
4 minutes
Makes 4

1 *15-ounce can chick peas (garbanzo beans), drained*
4 *green onions, coarsely chopped*
⅓ *cup parsley leaves*
2 *cloves garlic, chopped*
½ *teaspoon dried oregano, crushed*
¼ *teaspoon salt*
⅛ *teaspoon pepper*
all-purpose flour
1 *egg, lightly beaten*
½ *cup fine dry bread crumbs*
oil for shallow frying

4 *whole wheat bread rolls*
2 *tablespoons reduced-fat mayonnaise*
1 *cup alfalfa sprouts*

Ricotta Topping
½ *cup ricotta cheese*
1 *stalk celery, chopped*
1 *tablespoon seeded mustard*
2 *tablespoons fresh chopped chives*

1. Combine chick peas, green onions, parsley, garlic, and spices in food processor bowl or blender. Process for 10 seconds or until ingredients are just combined. Press ingredients together in the hands. Divide mixture into four, press into flat patties.
2. Dust patties with flour; shake off excess. Dip into egg; coat with bread crumbs.
3. Heat oil in a heavy-based skillet over medium-high heat. Add patties and cook 2 minutes on each side or until golden brown. Remove; drain on paper towels.
4. **To make Ricotta Topping:** Combine ricotta, celery, mustard and chives. Mix well. Split bread rolls in half, spread with mayonnaise. Top rolls with patties, ricotta topping and alfalfa sprouts. Serve.

Lamb Burgers with Cheese and Bacon (top) and Chick Pea and Ricotta Burgers.

Ham, Cheese and Pineapple English Muffins

Preparation time:
  15 minutes
Total cooking time:
  10 minutes
Makes 4

4 English muffins
2 tablespoons seeded
  mustard
1 tablespoon oil
1 leek, sliced
4 round ham slices
4 pineapple slices,
  drained
4 eggs
4 slices cheddar cheese

1. Split muffins in half crosswise and toast. Spread with mustard.
2. Heat oil in a skillet. Add leek and cook over medium heat 1 minute or until soft. Divide leek between four muffin halves.
3. Add ham slices to skillet; cook for 1 minute on each side or until lightly browned. Remove from skillet; place on top of leek. Repeat with pineapple.
4. Break eggs, one at a time, into a cup; slide into pan. Cook over low heat for 1 minute or until cooked as desired. Remove from skillet; place on top of pineapple. Place cheese on top of eggs. Place on a broiler rack. Broil 4 inches from the heat for 1 minute or until just melted. Top with remaining muffin halves. Serve.

Variation: You could use bagels instead of English muffins.

Sesame Pork Burgers

Preparation time:
  15 minutes
Total cooking time:
  10 minutes
Makes 4

1 pound ground pork
½ cup rolled oats
1 tablespoon sesame
  seeds
1 tablespoon soy sauce
2 cloves garlic, crushed
1 teaspoon grated fresh
  gingerroot
⅓ cup plum sauce
4 bread rolls

Topping
1 tablespoon sesame oil
½ red bell pepper,
  chopped
2 green onions,
  chopped
2 cups chopped bok
  choy

1. Combine pork in a medium bowl with oats, sesame seeds, soy sauce, garlic and gingerroot. Divide into four equal portions; shape into flat patties.
2. Place onto a cold, lightly oiled broiler pan. Brush with a little plum sauce. Broil 4 inches from the heat for 4 minutes on each side or until no longer pink. Brush burgers with plum sauce occasionally during cooking.
3. *To make Topping:* Heat sesame oil in a skillet; add bell peppers and onion. Cook over medium heat for 2 minutes or until tender. Add bok choy; cook and stir until just cooked. Remove from heat.
4. Split bread rolls in half; toast lightly. Top with burgers and spoon on topping. Serve.

HINT
Sesame oil, found in Asian shops and some supermarkets, has a strong, distinctive taste and gives the topping a toasted flavor. Peanut oil can be substituted for the sesame oil.

---

*Ham, Cheese and Pineapple English Muffins (top)
and Sesame Pork Burgers.*

Hot Chicken Rolls

Preparation time:
20 minutes
Total cooking time:
8 minutes
Serves 4

4 boneless, skinless
  chicken breasts
½ cup all-purpose flour
2 eggs, lightly beaten
1 cup fine dry bread
  crumbs
1 tablespoon Cajun
  seasoning blend
2 tablespoons oil
4 hamburger buns
4 lettuce leaves
½ cup creamy ranch
  dressing or mayonnaise

1. Trim chicken of
excess fat. Flatten each
fillet slightly with rolling
pin. Toss in flour; shake
off excess. Dip into egg,
then coat with
combined bread crumbs
and seasoning.
2. Heat oil in heavy-
based skillet; add
chicken. Cook over
medium heat 4 minutes
each side or until no
longer pink. Drain on
paper towels.
3. Place a lettuce leaf
on bottom half of each
bun. Top with chicken
and dollop of dressing.
Garnish with chives.

Herbed Chicken Patties

Preparation time:
10 minutes
Total cooking time:
12 minutes
Serves 4

1 pound ground
  chicken
1 cup fresh white bread
  crumbs
1 large onion, finely
  chopped
2 tablespoons chopped
  fresh chives
2 tablespoons chopped
  fresh parsley
1 tablespoon chopped
  fresh thyme
2 teaspoons
  Worcestershire sauce
1 egg, lightly beaten
3 ounces feta cheese,
  crumbled
freshly ground black
  pepper to taste
½ cup fruit chutney

1. Place ground
chicken in a bowl. Add
bread crumbs, onion,

chives, parsley, thyme,
Worcestershire sauce
and egg; stir until
combined.
2. Divide the mixture
into eight equal
portions and shape into
patties about ½ inch
thick.
3. Place patties on a
cold, lightly oiled
broiler pan. Broil 4
inches from the heat for
5 minutes on each side
or until browned and
no longer
pink.
4. Top each patty with
feta cheese and sprinkle
with pepper. Cook until
cheese has melted. Top
with a spoonful of
chutney. Patties may be
served in bread rolls if
desired.

Note: For convenience,
you can mix up the
patties a day ahead.
Keep them, covered, in
the refrigerator until
ready to cook.

HINT
To make a more
elaborate meal,
serve feta as a side
dish with the
patties. Combine
the feta with 1
tablespoon of
chopped mint, 2
tablespoons of olive
oil and 1
tablespoon of
lemon juice.

*Hot Chicken Rolls (top)
and Herbed Chicken Patties.*

Beef Tacos

Preparation time:
  20 minutes
Total cooking time:
  10 minutes
Serves 4

1 tablespoon oil
1 small onion, finely
  chopped
1 pound ground beef
1 ¼-ounce package
  taco seasoning mix
¼ cup water
½ cup taco sauce
8 taco shells
4 lettuce leaves, finely
  shredded
1 large tomato,
  chopped
1 cup shredded cheddar
  cheese

1. Heat oil in a skillet
over medium heat.
Add onion and cook
until soft. Add ground
beef and cook until
meat is brown. Drain
off fat.
2. Add seasoning mix,
water and taco sauce
to ground beef
mixture and stir over
medium heat for 3
minutes, or until
thickened.
3. To serve, place
some of the ground
beef mixture in the
base of each taco shell.
Top with lettuce,
tomato and shredded
cheese.

Beef and Bean Burritos

Preparation time:
  30 minutes
Total cooking time:
  30 minutes
Serves 4

2 tablespoons oil
1 medium onion, sliced
1 tablespoon ground
  cumin
2 teaspoons ground
  coriander
½ teaspoon ground
  cinnamon
1 teaspoon chili
  powder
1¼ pounds ground beef
1 14½-ounce can diced
  tomatoes
⅓ cup tomato paste
1 16-ounce can kidney
  beans, drained
1 8-ounce can corn
  kernels
8 6-inch flour tortillas

Topping
1½ cups shredded
cheddar cheese
¼ cup taco sauce,
  optional

1. Heat oil in a large
skillet; add onion,
spices and ground beef.
Cook over medium-
high heat for 10
minutes until well
browned and almost all
the liquid has
evaporated. Use a fork
to break up any lumps
of meat as it cooks.
Drain off fat. Reduce
heat to low. Add
tomatoes and paste.
Cover and cook,
stirring occasionally,
for 20 minutes. Add
kidney beans and corn
and stir until heated
through.
2. Preheat oven to
350°F. To assemble
burritos, place about ½
cup of beef mixture on
each tortilla. Roll
tortillas around filling
and place, seam-side
down, in a shallow
baking dish. (Allow
two burritos per
person.) Sprinkle with
shredded cheese and
bake for 10 minutes or
until the cheese has
melted. Top each burrito
with a tablespoon of
taco sauce, if desired,
and serve immediately,
with a green salad.

Note: Flour tortillas are
available in
supermarkets near the
bread or in the
refrigerated section.

Beef Tacos (top) **and** *Beef and Bean Burritos.*

Nachos with Guacamole

Preparation time:
  20 minutes
Total cooking time:
  3–5 minutes
Serves 4

1 16-ounce can red
  kidney beans, rinsed
  and drained
⅓ cup bottled salsa
8 ounces tortilla
  chips
2 cups shredded
  cheddar cheese
1½ cups bottled salsa,
  extra
⅓ cup sour cream

Guacamole
1 large avocado
1 green onion, finely
  chopped
1 small tomato, finely
  chopped
1 tablespoon lemon
  juice
freshly ground black
  pepper to taste

1. Preheat oven to
moderate 350°F.
Combine kidney beans
and salsa; divide the
mixture between four
ovenproof serving
plates. Cover with
tortilla chips and
cheese. Place in oven
and cook for 3–5

minutes or until cheese
has melted.
2. To assemble nachos,
spoon extra salsa onto
melted cheese; top with
guacamole and sour
cream.
3. *To make
Guacamole:* Peel and
pit avocado. Mash
flesh lightly with a
fork, and combine
with green onion,
tomato, lemon juice
and pepper.

Lamb Mini Meatballs with Hot Red Sauce

Preparation time:
  25 minutes
Total cooking time:
  15 minutes
Makes about 10

1½ pounds ground lamb
1 small onion, finely
  chopped
¼ cup finely chopped
  parsley
1 tablespoon Dijon
  mustard

Hot Red Sauce
2 large red bell peppers
1 tablespoon tarragon
  vinegar
¼ cup pine nuts
2 cloves garlic, crushed
¼ teaspoon finely
  chopped chili peppers
¼ cup olive oil

1. Place lamb, onion,
parsley and mustard in
a large mixing bowl
and combine
thoroughly. Roll level
tablespoonfuls of
mixture into 40 balls.
Refrigerate until
required. Thread four
meatballs onto each of
10 skewers.
2. *To make Hot Red
Sauce:* Cut bell pepper
in half and remove
seeds. Place pepper,
skin-side up, under
broiler and broil until
skin is black. Place in a
paper bag; seal and
cool. Rub off skin.
Place roasted pepper,
vinegar, pine nuts,
garlic and chili pepper
in a food processor or
blender. Process at
medium speed, adding
oil slowly until
smooth. Pour into
serving bowl.
3. Place skewers on a
broiler pan. Broil 4
inches from heat about
12 minutes or until
well browned, turning
once. Drain on paper
towels and serve with
Hot Red Sauce.

*Nachos with Guacamole (top) and Lamb Mini
Meatballs with Hot Red Sauce.*

Chili Sausage Dogs

Preparation time:
  20 minutes
Total cooking time:
  10 minutes
Makes 4

1 medium tomato,
  finely chopped
1 small red onion,
  finely chopped
2 teaspoons sweet chili
  sauce
1 tablespoon finely
  chopped fresh basil
2 teaspoons oil
4 herb-and-garlic-
  flavored sausages
4 long bread rolls

1. Place tomato, onion, chili sauce and basil in a small bowl; mix well.
2. Heat oil in a skillet. Prick the sausages all over with a fork; cook over medium heat for 10 minutes or until they are brown and fully cooked.
3. Cut a deep slit along top of each roll. Place a sausage in the opening; top with some of the tomato/chili mixture. Serve immediately.

Note: You can use any of your favorite sausages.

Glazed Apricot Ribs

Preparation time:
  5 minutes
Total cooking time:
  2 hours
Serves 4

3 pounds beef spareribs
½ cup apricot nectar
1 tablespoon soy sauce
1 tablespoon sweet chili
  sauce
2 cloves garlic, crushed
2 teaspoons grated
  fresh gingerroot

1. Preheat oven to moderately low 325°F. Place the spareribs in a single layer in a baking dish.
2. Combine apricot nectar, soy sauce, chili sauce, garlic and gingerroot and pour over the spareribs.
3. Bake for 1½–2 hours or until ribs are tender and well-browned, brushing occasionally with glaze during cooking. Serve.

HINT
The spareribs will have more flavor if you have time to marinate them in the glaze for several hours.

Chili Sausage Dogs (top) and Glazed Apricot Ribs.

Chicken Sausage Dogs

Preparation time:
 30 minutes
Total cooking time
 5–10 minutes
Serves 4

Chicken Sausages
1 pound ground
 chicken
1 cup fresh bread
 crumbs
1/3 cup fruit chutney
3 cloves garlic, crushed
1/4 teaspoon fennel
 seeds, crushed
1/2 cup soft cream
 cheese
1/2 cup chopped chives
8 large flour tortillas

Filling
1 small apple, finely
 chopped
1 medium tomato,
 finely chopped
1/2 red onion, finely
 chopped
2 tablespoons lemon
 juice

1. **To make Chicken Sausages:** Combine ground chicken, bread crumbs, chutney, garlic, and fennel; divide into eight equal portions. Roll each portion into a sausage shape about 5 inches long. Place onto an oiled, unheated broiler rack. Broil 4 inches from the heat for 5–10 minutes or until cooked through; turn sausages occasionally. Drain on paper towels. Keep warm.
2. Combine cream cheese and chives; spread over tortillas.
3. **To make Filling:** Combine apple, tomato, onion and lemon juice. Spoon onto one side of tortillas.
4. Place sausages onto tortillas with filling. Roll tortillas to enclose filling; secure with toothpicks. Serve.

Club Sandwiches

Preparation time:
 15 minutes
Total cooking time:
 None
Serves 4

12 slices bread

Tuna Filling
1 6½-ounce can tuna,
 drained

1 tablespoon mayonnaise
1/2 teaspoon curry
 powder
8 gherkins, sliced
 lengthwise

Salad
1/2 head iceberg lettuce
1 large tomato, sliced
1 cucumber, sliced

1. In a small bowl, combine the tuna, mayonnaise and curry powder.
2. Spread four slices of bread with tuna filling and top with gherkin slices. Top each with a slice of bread.
3. Arrange lettuce, tomato and cucumber in layers and top with remaining bread.
4. Cut sandwiches diagonally in half; insert a toothpick in each to hold the layers in place.

Variation: The bread may be toasted, if you prefer. Other fillings may be used: curried egg salad, sliced roast beef and chutney, or chicken and avocado or bacon.

HINT
Sandwiches are best made just before serving. If you have to make them ahead, cover with a clean damp towel and refrigerate.

Chicken Sausage Dogs (top) and Club Sandwiches.

Cut pastry into rounds and press into muffin cups.

For filling, cook ground beef until well browned. Use a fork to break up lumps.

Meat Pies

Preparation time:
  20 minutes
Total cooking time:
  15–20 minutes
Makes 16

2 15-ounce packages
  folded, refrigerated,
  unbaked pie crusts (4)
2 small tomatoes,
  sliced
½ teaspoon dried
  oregano, crushed

Filling
1 pound ground beef
1 onion, chopped
2 cloves garlic,
  crushed
3 tablespoons
  all-purpose flour
1½ cups beef stock
⅓ cup tomato
  sauce
1 tablespoon
  Worcestershire sauce

1 tablespoon chopped
  fresh rosemary

1. Preheat oven to moderately hot 425°F. Cut pastry into 16 circles using a round, 4-inch fluted cutter. Press pastry circles into muffin cups (½-cup capacity).

2. *To make Filling:* In a heavy-based saucepan cook ground beef, onion and garlic over medium heat until meat is brown and onion is tender. Use a fork to break up any lumps of ground beef as it cooks. Drain off fat.

3. Add flour; stir until combined. Cook over medium heat for 1 minute. Add stock, sauces and rosemary; cook and stir until bubbly. Reduce heat to low; simmer for 5 minutes or until mixture has reduced and thickened; stir occasionally. Remove pan from heat; allow to cool.

4. Divide the filling between the pastry shells. Top each with a slice of tomato and sprinkle with oregano. Bake for 15–20 minutes or until pastry is golden brown and crisp. Serve warm.

HINT
To make traditional meat pies, follow the recipe up to the last step and cut out rounds of pastry to fit the top. Place the pastry rounds over the tomato and oregano topping; seal edges and brush with beaten egg. Bake until the pastry is puffed and golden.

Meat Pies.

Cook filling mixture until it has reduced and thickened, stirring occasionally.

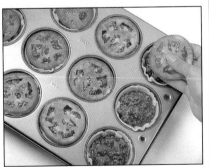

Fill pastry shells and top each with a slice of tomato and sprinkling of oregano.

San Choy Bow

Preparation time:
  10 minutes
Total cooking time:
  10 minutes
Serves 4

1 tablespoon oil
1 onion, chopped
1 small red bell pepper,
  chopped
1 clove garlic, crushed
1 teaspoon hot chili
  sauce
6 ounces ground pork
1 cup coconut milk
2 tablespoons peanut
  butter
1 tablespoon lemon
  juice
2 teaspoons soy sauce
8 lettuce cups

1. Heat oil in a large skillet over medium heat. Add onion, bell pepper, garlic and chili sauce. Cook and stir for 2 minutes or until onion is soft.
2. Add pork and cook over high heat for 3 minutes or until well browned and almost all the liquid has evaporated. Use a fork to break up any lumps of meat as it cooks. Drain off fat.
3. Add coconut milk, peanut butter, lemon juice and soy sauce. Bring to a boil; reduce heat to low. Simmer,

uncovered, for 5 minutes or until almost all the liquid has evaporated. Remove from heat; cool.
4. Spoon mixture into lettuce cups to serve.

Variation: You can use ground chicken or beef instead of pork.

Tandoori Chicken Pockets

Preparation time:
  15 minutes
Total cooking time:
  7 minutes
Serves 4

½ cup plain yogurt
2 tablespoons tandoori
  paste (see Hint)
4 boneless, skinless
  chicken thighs
4 pita bread pockets

Filling
1 cucumber, chopped
1 medium tomato,
  peeled, seeded,
  chopped

2 tablespoons plain
  yogurt, extra
2 tablespoons flaked
  coconut
2 tablespoons chopped
  fresh mint

1. Combine yogurt and tandoori paste in a medium bowl. Add chicken; stir until chicken is well coated.
2. Place chicken on an unheated, lightly oiled broiler rack. Broil 4 inches from the heat for 3 minutes on each side or until cooked through. Cool chicken; slice thinly.
3. Broil pita pockets 4 inches from heat for 1 minute or until heated through.
4. *To make Filling:* Combine cucumber, tomato, extra yogurt, coconut and mint.
5. Cut pita pockets crosswise in half; fill cavities with chicken and filling. Serve immediately.

HINT
Tandoori paste is an Indian blend of hot and fragrant spices including turmeric, paprika, chili powder, saffron, cardamom and garam masala.

---

*San Choy Bow (top)
and Tandoori Chicken Pockets.*

Salmon Pita Pockets

Preparation time:
10 minutes
Total cooking time:
None
Makes 4

Mayonnaise
egg substitute
  equivalent to 1 egg
1/2 teaspoon prepared
  mustard
1 tablespoon lime juice
2/3 cup olive oil
salt and white pepper
  to taste

2 6½-ounce cans
  boneless, skinless
  salmon, drained
3 ounces mixed salad
  greens
1 medium tomato, sliced
4 pita bread pockets

1. Place egg substitute
in a small mixing bowl,
add mustard and half
the lime juice. Beat with
electric beaters until light
and creamy. Gradually
add oil, beating
constantly until mixture
is thick and creamy.
2. Increase addition of
oil as the mayonnaise
thickens. Continue
beating until all the oil
is added. Stir in
remaining juice, and

salt and pepper to taste.
3. Flake salmon with a
fork. Place salad greens
and tomato into pocket
breads; top with salmon
and mayonnaise. Serve
immediately.

Lamb and Onion Sandwiches

Preparation time:
  5 minutes
Total cooking time:
  10 minutes
Serves 4

2 tablespoons oil
2 large onions, sliced in
  rings
4 eggs
1 pound boneless lamb
  cutlets
1 tablespoon
  Worcestershire sauce
8 slices bread
2 tablespoons tomato
  sauce
2 medium ripe
  tomatoes, sliced
1 8-ounce can sliced
  beets, well drained

Salmon Pita Pockets (top) and
Lamb and Onion Sandwiches.

1. Heat the oil in a
large skillet over a
medium heat. Add the
sliced onions and cook
them for 3 minutes or
until tender and brown;
remove from pan.
2. Break the eggs into a
cup, one at a time, and
slide them into the
skillet. Cook until
desired doneness.
Remove the eggs from
the pan, and keep them
warm.
3. Add the lamb cutlets
to the skillet; cook
them for 1–2 minutes
on each side. Add the
Worcestershire sauce;
allow the sauce to coat
the cutlets and then
remove them from the
skillet.
4. Toast the bread
slices. Spread four slices
with tomato sauce; top
with the onions, eggs,
lamb, sliced tomatoes
and beets. Place the
remaining toast on
top. Slice diagonally.
Serve.

Note: If you can't find
boneless lamb cutlets,
substitute veal cutlets
instead. Pound the
cutlets slightly with a
meat mallet to flatten
them. To make a
traditional beef steak
sandwich, use slices of
beef tenderloin or very
thin slices of boneless
round steak instead of
the lamb.

Potato Wedges with Herb Dip

Preparation time:
  15 minutes
Total cooking time:
  4 minutes
Serves 4

2 pounds baking
  potatoes
oil for deep-frying

Creamy Herb Dip
½ cup sour cream
2 tablespoons plain
  yogurt
2 tablespoons chopped
  chives
1 tablespoon chopped
  fresh thyme
1 clove garlic, crushed
1 teaspoon sweet chili
  sauce (optional)

1. Peel potatoes and
cut each into about 10
wedges. Dry wedges
with paper towels.
2. Heat oil in a deep
heavy-based saucepan
to 375°F. Gently lower
potato wedges into hot
oil. Cook for 4 minutes
or until golden brown.
Remove from oil; drain
on paper towels.
3. *To make Creamy
Herb Dip:* Combine
sour cream and yogurt.
Mix in chives, thyme,
garlic and chili sauce, if
desired. Serve as dip
with warm potato
wedges.

French Fries

Preparation time:
  20 minutes
Total cooking time:
  6 minutes
Serves 4

4 medium baking
  potatoes
oil for deep-frying
salt, to taste

1. Peel potatoes; rinse
and pat dry with paper
towels. Cut lengthwise
into ¼-inch wide strips.
Then cut each piece
into ¼-inch wide fries.
2. Heat oil in a deep,
heavy-based pan to
375°F. Gently lower
fries, a few at a time,
into the oil. Cook for
5–6 minutes or until
light brown and crisp.
Carefully remove with
tongs. Drain on paper
towels. Repeat with
remaining potatoes.
Sprinkle with salt.
3. To reheat fries, place
in a single layer on a
baking sheet. Bake in a
300°F oven until hot.

Note: To make
shoestring potatoes,
prepare as above, except
cut potatoes into long
thin strips and fry for
3–4 minutes.

French Loaf Grill

Preparation time:
  10 minutes
Total cooking time:
  3 minutes
Makes 8

¼ cup butter, softened
1 clove garlic, crushed
1 tablespoon whole
  grain mustard
2 teaspoons lemon
  juice
8 thick slices French
  bread
1 15-ounce can
  asparagus spears
4 slices ham
3 ounces gruyère
  cheese, sliced

1. Place butter, garlic,
mustard and lemon
juice in a small bowl;
mix well. Spread one
side of French bread
slices with the butter
mixture.
2. Drain asparagus
spears thoroughly. Lay
on buttered side of
bread; top with ham
and cheese slice.
3. Place sandwiches on
an unheated broiler
rack. Broil 4 inches
from the heat about 3
minutes or until cheese
has melted. Serve
warm.

*From top: French Fries, French Loaf Grill and
Potato Wedges with Herb Dip.*

Chicken Phyllo Parcels

Preparation time:
 20 minutes
Total cooking time:
 20 minutes
Makes 6

1 *whole cooked chicken*
12 *sheets frozen phyllo dough, thawed*
¼ *cup oil*
1 *large avocado, sliced*
2 *small tomatoes, sliced*
1 *cup shredded cheddar cheese*
3 *green onions, finely sliced*
2 *tablespoons butter, melted*

1. Preheat oven to 425°F. Brush baking sheet with oil. Remove meat from chicken. Shred meat.
2. Lay one sheet of phyllo dough on work surface, short edge to front; brush lightly with oil. Top with second sheet. Place one-sixth of chicken in oblong pile about 4 inches in from end and 2 inches in from sides. Lay slices of avocado and tomato on top; sprinkle with cheese and onions.
3. Fold end of dough over filling; tuck in sides and roll up to form a parcel. Brush with butter. Repeat with remaining ingredients. Bake 20 minutes. Serve.

Pork Sausages in Pita

Preparation time:
 15 minutes
Total cooking time:
 8 minutes
Serves 4

1 *pound ground pork sausage*
⅓ *cup shredded apple*
2 *green onions, finely chopped*
2 *cabbage leaves, finely shredded*
4 *pita bread pockets*
⅓ *cup plum sauce*

1. Place sausage, apple and onion in bowl. Using hands, combine thoroughly. Divide mixture into four and form into patties.
2. Place patties in a skillet and cook over medium heat for 8 minutes or until thoroughly cooked, turning occasionally.
3. Divide cabbage between pita bread; place meat on top and drizzle with plum sauce.

Chicken Phyllo Parcels (left) and Pork Sausages in Pita.

Spicy Chicken Pastries

Preparation time:
20 minutes
Total cooking time:
30 minutes
Makes 8

1 tablespoon oil
1 small onion, finely
  chopped
1 clove garlic, crushed
1 teaspoon curry powder
1/8 teaspoon cayenne
  pepper
5 ounces ground chicken
1/4 cup frozen tiny peas
2 teaspoons finely
  chopped cilantro
2 15-ounce packages
  folded, refrigerated,
  unbaked pie crusts (4)
1 egg, lightly beaten

1. Preheat oven to moderate 350°F. Heat oil in a heavy-based skillet over medium heat. Add onion and cook 2 minutes, or until onion is soft. Add garlic, curry powder and pepper; cook and stir 1 minute more.
2. Add chicken to skillet; cook for 8 minutes or until chicken is no longer pink and almost all the liquid has evaporated. Use a fork to break up any lumps of chicken as it cooks. Stir in peas and cilantro; transfer to a bowl to cool.

3. Using a plate as a guide, cut 5-inch circles from pastry. Divide chicken mixture between each circle; fold over and flute edges to seal. Place on a baking sheet and brush with beaten egg. Bake 20 minutes or until golden. Serve warm or cool.

Ham and Cheese Croissants with Mustard Cream

Preparation time:
10 minutes
Total cooking time:
5 minutes
Serves 4

4 purchased croissants
4 slices Swiss cheese
4 slices ham

Mustard Cream
1/3 cup mayonnaise
1 tablespoon sour
  cream
1 teaspoon whole grain
  mustard

1. Preheat oven to moderate 350°F. Slice croissants in half horizontally. Lay a slice of Swiss cheese on each base; place on a baking sheet. Place croissant tops, cut-side down, on baking sheet. Cook for 5 minutes or until cheese has melted and croissants are crisp.
2. Place ham on top of cheese; spread mustard cream on ham and replace top of croissant. Serve immediately.
3. **To make Mustard Cream:** Place the mayonnaise, sour cream and mustard in a small bowl and mix well.

Note: You can buy croissants fresh from the bakery, or from the supermarket. They freeze very successfully.

HINT
Croissants are specially suitable for brunch entertaining. Other filling ideas are: camembert and avocado; chicken with thinly sliced mushrooms and sour cream; smoked salmon with sour cream and capers.

Spicy Chicken Pastries (top) and Ham and Cheese Croissants with Mustard Cream.

Fried Chicken

Preparation time:
 20 minutes
Total cooking time:
 10 minutes
Serves 4

8 chicken drumsticks
2 cups corn flakes
1 cup fine dry bread
 crumbs
½ cup all-purpose flour
2 eggs, beaten
oil for deep-frying
1 cup bottled salsa or
 taco sauce

1. Remove skin from drumsticks. Cook in a large pot of lightly salted water for 20 minutes or until just tender. Drain, cool, and pat dry.
2. Place corn flakes and bread crumbs in a food processor. Process for 20 seconds or until corn flakes are crushed and mixture is combined.
3. Working one at a time, dip drumsticks in flour, then egg. Coat well with crumb mixture. Heat oil in a deep, heavy-based pan to 365°F. Gently lower drumsticks into hot oil. Cook for 2–3 minutes or until crisp and golden. Carefully remove and drain on paper towels. Serve with salsa.

Chicken Salad Roll-ups

Preparation time:
 15 minutes
Total cooking time:
 5 minutes
Serves 4

1 pound boneless,
 skinless chicken thighs
1 tablespoon olive oil
1 small onion, sliced
4 large flour tortillas
½ cup mayonnaise
4 lettuce leaves, finely
 shredded
2 small tomatoes,
 chopped
½ small cucumber,
 sliced

1. Trim chicken of excess fat. Cut into thin strips. Heat oil in a skillet over medium heat; add chicken and onion and cook for 5 minutes or until golden and cooked through.
2. Lay tortillas out flat. Divide chicken mixture into four portions and place one portion in a pile at the end of each tortilla. Top with mayonnaise, lettuce, tomato and cucumber.
3. Fold end of bread over filling; tuck in sides and roll up. Serve immediately.

Chicken Salad Roll-ups (left) and Fried Chicken.

Chicken Nuggets with Sweet and Sour Sauce

Preparation time:
 20 minutes
Total cooking time:
 12 minutes
Serves 4

1 pound boneless,
 skinless chicken breasts
²⁄₃ cup all-purpose flour
1 egg, lightly beaten
1 cup corn flake crumbs

Sweet and Sour Sauce
¹⁄₃ cup orange juice
¹⁄₃ cup pineapple juice
¹⁄₃ cup white vinegar
¹⁄₄ cup brown sugar
1 tablespoon sweet chili
 sauce
2 teaspoons cornstarch
1 tablespoon water

1. Preheat oven to moderate 350°F. Line a baking sheet with foil. Cut chicken into rough 1-inch cubes. Working a few at a time, dip pieces in flour and shake off excess. Dip into egg; coat with corn flake crumbs. If you have time, refrigerate for 30 minutes.
2. Place nuggets on baking sheet and bake for 10–15 minutes until crisp and golden, Serve with sweet and sour sauce.

3. *To make Sweet and Sour Sauce:* Place juices, vinegar, sugar and chili sauce in a small pan. Stir over medium heat until sugar has dissolved. Combine cornstarch and water in a small bowl until smooth; add to pan. Stir over medium heat until mixture boils and thickens. Reduce heat and simmer for 2 minutes. Transfer to a small bowl to cool. Serve warm or at room temperature.

Spanish Omelette

Preparation time:
 20 minutes
Total cooking time:
 25 minutes
Serves 6

2 pounds baking
 potatoes
1 tablespoon olive oil
1 large onion, finely
 chopped
2–3 ounces sliced
 salami, chopped
4 eggs, lightly beaten

1. Cut potatoes into rough ¾-inch cubes and cook in a large pan of boiling water until just tender. Drain and cool.
2. Heat oil in a 10-inch non-stick skillet over medium-low heat. Add onion and cook for 3 minutes or until soft. Add salami and cook 3 minutes more, stirring occasionally.
3. Add potatoes to pan, and cook for 5 minutes, stirring to combine. Try to distribute onion and salami through the potato, so that they are not all on the base of pan. Reduce heat to low; preheat broiler.
4. Pour eggs into pan, moving potato mixture to let eggs flow through. Cook for 3 minutes, until egg has set around edges and base. Remove pan from the stove top and broil 4 inches from the heat for 2–3 minutes until the top has set. Invert onto a plate and cut into wedges. Serve warm or at room temperature.

Note: For a different flavor, add some chopped bell pepper with the onion.

Chicken Nuggets with Sweet and Sour Sauce (top) and Spanish Omelette.

Rub butter into flour until the mixture is fine and crumbly.

Roll dough out to a rectangle and spread with tomato paste.

Pizza Wheels

Preparation time:
  25 minutes
Total cooking time:
  25–30 minutes
Serves 4

2 cups all-purpose flour
1 teaspoon baking
  powder
¼ teaspoon salt
3 tablespoons butter,
  chopped
½ cup milk
¼ cup tomato paste
¼ cup finely chopped
  onion
¼ cup chopped ham
2 pineapple slices,
  finely chopped
½ cup shredded
  cheddar cheese
1 tablespoon finely
  chopped parsley

1. Preheat oven to
350°F. Brush baking
sheet with oil. Stir
together flour, baking
powder and salt. Rub
butter into flour mixture
until fine and crumbly.
Add all the milk and mix
to soft dough, adding
more milk if necessary.
Turn onto lightly
floured surface and
knead for 30 seconds.
2. Roll out dough onto
parchment or waxed
paper to a 12 x 8-inch
rectangle, about ⅛ inch
thick. Spread tomato
paste over dough,
leaving ¼-inch edge.
3. Combine onion, ham,
pineapple, cheese and
parsley. Spread over
tomato paste, leaving
1-inch edge. Using
paper as a guide, roll up
dough from long side.
4. Cut roll into eight
slices. Place slices, cut
side down, on baking
sheet. Bake 25–30
minutes or until golden.

Pizza Wheels.

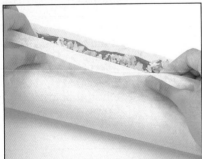

*Using paper as a guide, roll up dough
from long side.*

*Cut roll into eight slices and place cut
side down on baking sheet.*

55

Fish in Beer Batter with Tartar Sauce

Preparation time:
  15 minutes +
  15minutes resting
Total cooking time:
  6 minutes
Serves 4

2 cups all-purpose flour
1 egg, lightly beaten
1¼ cups flat beer
1¼ pounds boneless
  fish fillets
oil for deep-frying

Tartar Sauce
⅔ cup mayonnaise
1 tablespoon chopped
  capers
1 tablespoon chopped
  gherkins
1 tablespoon finely
  chopped parsley
1 teaspoon lemon juice

1. Sift flour into a large bowl; make a well in the center. Add egg and beer all at once; whisk until all liquid is incorporated and batter is free of lumps. Leave, covered with plastic wrap, for 15 minutes.
2. Heat oil in large heavy-based pan to 365°F. Pat fish dry. Dip fish into batter, then gently lower into hot oil. Cook for 3–4 minutes, until golden and crisp. Carefully remove from oil with tongs or slotted spoon. Drain on paper towels. Serve immediately with tartar sauce.
3. *To make Tartar Sauce:* Combine mayonnaise, capers, gherkins, parsley and lemon juice in small mixing bowl.

Note: When deep-frying, the pan should only be half full of oil, as the level will rise while cooking. Cook one or two pieces of fish at a time.

Eggplant and Pepper Grill

Preparation time:
  15 minutes
Total cooking time:
  8 minutes
Serves 4

2 tablespoons oil
1 small pepper, cut into
  ¼-inch slices
1 large focaccia bread
  (12 x 12 inch)

½ cup tomato paste
1 small onion, finely
  sliced
1 small red bell pepper,
  cut into thin strips
¼ cup chopped cilantro
⅔ cup shredded
  mozzarella cheese
⅓ cup shredded
  Parmesan cheese

1. Heat oil in a large skillet over medium heat. Cook eggplant slices for 2 minutes or until soft and just golden. Drain on paper towels.
2. Cut focaccia into four squares, then in half horizontally. Toast each side for 2 minutes, until golden. Spread with tomato paste.
3. Place eggplant, onion, bell pepper, cilantro and combined cheeses on base of each square. Broil 4 inches from heat for 2–3 minutes or until cheese has melted. Serve immediately.

HINT
Almost anything is suitable as focaccia bread topping: try chicken, ham, sliced tomatoes or avocado. Cover your topping with cheese and melt under the broiler.

---

*Fish in Beer Batter with Tartar Sauce (top)
and Eggplant and Pepper Grill.*

Grilled Ham and Cheese Sandwiches

Preparation time:
10 minutes
Total cooking time:
3–5 minutes
Makes 4

8 slices white bread
2 tablespoons soft butter
4 slices ham
1 large tomato, sliced
4 slices American cheese
black pepper, to taste

1. Preheat griddle or large skillet over medium heat. Spread one side of each bread slice with butter. Place bread, buttered side down, on work surface.
2. Place a slice of ham on four of the unbuttered slices of bread. Top with tomato and cheese. Sprinkle with pepper. Top with remaining bread, buttered side out.
3. Place sandwiches on griddle and cook 2–3 minutes or until bread is toasted and cheese has melted, turning once. Cut in half and serve warm.

Note: Grilled ham and cheese sandwiches can be made with a toasted sandwich maker. Follow the manufacturer's directions for toasting the sandwiches. Custom-make your grilled sandwich by choosing from a variety of cheeses, such as cheddar, Swiss, Colby or Monterey Jack. You can omit the ham to make a cheese sandwich or use roast beef, turkey, chicken, Canadian bacon, or cooked bacon

strips. Or, add onions, peppers and avocadoes and serve with potato chips, a fresh green salad or tomato soup.

Pepperoni Pizza

Preparation time:
25 minutes
Total cooking time:
15–20 minutes
Serves 4–6

2 cups all-purpose flour
1 teaspoon baking powder
1/4 teaspoon salt
3 tablespoons butter, chopped
1 cup shredded mozzarella cheese
1/2 cup milk
1/2 cup chunky spaghetti sauce
1/2 small onion, finely sliced
1 1/2 ounces pepperoni, cut into thin strips
1 2 1/4-ounce can sliced black pitted olives
1/3 cup shredded Parmesan cheese

1. Preheat oven to moderately hot 425°F. Brush a baking sheet with oil. Set aside.
2. Place flour, baking powder and salt in a food processor bowl. Add butter and cheese. Using the pulse action, process for 30 seconds or until mixture is fine and crumbly. Add all the milk and process 30 seconds more or until mixture comes together, adding more liquid if necessary.
3. Turn mixture onto a lightly floured surface. Knead lightly for 2 minutes or until smooth. Roll out dough to 12 x 8-inch rectangle; place in prepared baking sheet. Spread the dough with sauce and top with onion, pepperoni, olives and Parmesan cheese. Bake for 15–20 minutes or until crust is brown and topping is heated through. Cut into rectangles to serve. Serve warm.

Grilled Ham and Cheese Sandwich (top) and Pepperoni Pizza.

Calzones

Preparation time:
 30 minutes
Total cooking time:
 20 minutes
Serves 4

3 cups all-purpose flour
½ teaspoon salt
1 egg, lightly beaten
⅔ cup buttermilk
½ cup butter, melted
⅔ cup bottled spaghetti
 sauce
2 ounces sliced salami
4 ounces fresh
 mushrooms, sliced
1 6-ounce jar marinated
 artichoke hearts,
 drained and sliced
¼ cup fresh basil leaves
4 ounces fresh mozzarella
 cheese, sliced
⅓ cup shredded
 Parmesan cheese
milk for glazing
2 tablespoons cornmeal

1. Preheat oven to moderately hot 425°F. Brush two baking sheets lightly with melted butter or oil. Place flour and salt into a large mixing bowl; add the combined egg, buttermilk and butter. Mix to a soft dough. Turn onto a lightly floured surface, knead for 1 minute or until smooth.
2. Divide the mixture in half and roll each half into a 12-inch circle.
3. Divide the spaghetti sauce, salami, mushrooms, artichokes, basil, mozzarella cheese and Parmesan cheese between the circles of dough, placing ingredients on one half of each circle, leaving a ¾-inch border.
4. Brush border of each circle with milk. Fold dough over the top to enclose the filling; press the edges together to seal and flute the edges. Brush top of dough with milk; sprinkle with cornmeal. Place on oven baking sheets. Bake for 20 minutes or until golden brown.

Note: These covered pizzas can be assembled 1 hour in advance and stored in the refrigerator. Cook them just before serving.

HINT
Balls of fresh mozzarella cheese can be found in health food stores, some large supermarkets, or specialty food shops. They will keep, covered with water, in the refrigerator for a few days. Change the water daily.

Calzones.

Add egg, buttermilk and butter to flour; mix to a soft dough.

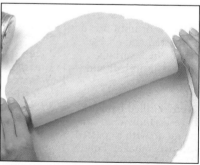

Divide dough in half and roll out to two 12-inch circles.

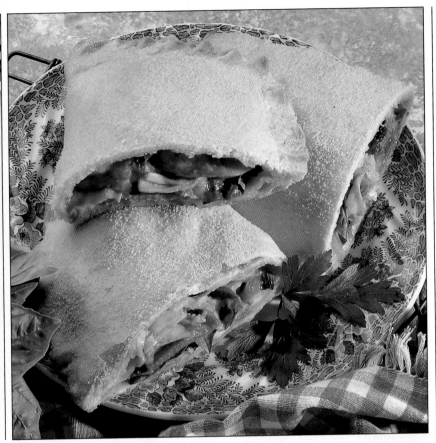

Divide sauce, salami, mushrooms, basil, artichokes and cheeses between circles.

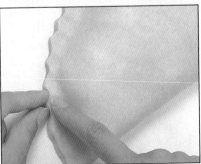

Press the edges of the dough together to seal and flute edges.

61

Mini Vegetarian Pizzas

Preparation time:
 20 minutes
Total cooking time:
 20 minutes
Serves 4

1 tablespoon oil
1 small green bell
 pepper, cut into short
 thin strips
5 ounces mushrooms,
 thinly sliced
1 medium zucchini,
 thinly sliced
4 mini pizza crusts
2/3 cup purchased
 meatless spaghetti sauce
1 14-ounce can
 artichoke hearts,
 drained and quartered
1 7-ounce can corn
 kernels, drained
1 cup shredded
 mozzarella cheese

1. Preheat oven to
moderately hot 425°F.
Brush two baking
sheets lightly with
melted butter or oil.
Heat oil in a skillet
over medium heat. Add
bell pepper, mushrooms
and zucchini and cook
for 3 minutes, or until
they are soft. Cool.
2. Spread pizza crusts
with spaghetti sauce.
Top with the cooked
vegetables, artichokes
and corn. Sprinkle with
cheese.
3. Place on prepared
baking sheets and bake
for 15–20 minutes or
until cheese has melted
and crusts are crisp.

Note: Pita bread, flour
tortillas or other flat
breads also make good
crusts for pizza
toppings.

Sausage Rolls

Preparation time:
 20 minutes
Total cooking time:
 35–40 minutes
Makes 8

1 pound ground pork
 sausage
1/4 grated onion
2 tablespoons barbecue
 sauce
1/4 cup fine dry bread
 crumbs
1 15-ounce package
 folded, refrigerated
 unbaked pie crusts (2)
1 egg, lightly beaten

1. Preheat oven to
moderate 350°F. Line a
baking sheet with
aluminum foil. Brush
the foil with oil.
2. Combine ground
sausage, onion,
barbecue sauce and
bread crumbs in a
medium mixing bowl.
Using your hands, mix
until well combined.
3. Roll each round pie
crust into a 12 x 9-inch
rectangle. Cut each
rectangle in half
lengthwise. Divide the
meat mixture into four
equal portions. Place
one portion lengthwise
down the center of each
pastry strip. Roll up
and brush edges with
egg to seal.
4. With seam-side
down, cut each roll
crosswise in half. Place
on baking sheet. Bake
for 35–40 minutes or
until pastry is crisp and
golden and sausage is
thoroughly cooked.
Serve with tomato sauce.

Note: This recipe is for
large sausage rolls. For
a party, they can be cut
into smaller portions.
Serve them with tomato
sauce, or try a bottled
sweet chili sauce.

*Mini Vegetarian Pizzas (top)
and Sausage Rolls.*

Index